TEACHER'S GUIDE

ORION
SERIES

Contents

Lesson 1: Under Attack   Theme—Perseverance 2

Lesson 2: First Encounter   Theme—Courage 8

Lesson 3: Betrayed   Theme—Respect 14

Lesson 4: Deception   Theme—Integrity 20

Lesson 5: Countdown   Theme—Responsibility 26

Skill Masters

Literary Response

Comprehension

D1385019

Steck Vaughn™

A Harcourt Achieve Imprint

> "The graphic novel is being recognized for its contribution to the development of both visual and verbal literacy . . . to fully grasp the meaning of the story."
>
> – Michelle Gorman, *Getting Graphic! Using Graphic Novels to Promote Literacy with Preteens and Teens*

Impact Graphic Novels for Your Struggling Readers

- Readers can identify with the characters who overcome fears and insecurities, deal with family and social conflicts, and learn to contribute to those around them.

- Your students will learn core character values as they're engaged in the high-interest, visually stimulating novels.

- Watch as your struggling readers become motivated to thinking critically about a story as they practice key comprehension and literary response skills.

Impact Graphic Novels look and read like the popular graphic novels in bookstores today!

Your students won't get enough of these exciting stories!

VERSUS

Top high school athletes tour the world in an international sports competition.

SHADOWCAST

A group of strangers are lost on a mysterious, deserted island and have to work together to find their way home.

ORION

This series of books follows a secret task force of superpowered teens as they travel through space to save the world from alien invaders. The characters in *Orion* learn . . .

Integrity

Courage

Perseverance

Responsibility

Respect

> "When teachers bring to the fore the character dimension of the curriculum, they enhance the relevance of subject matter ... and in the process, increase student engagement and achievement."
>
> – Tom Lickona, *Eleven Principles of Effective Character Education*

Fun Books, Valuable Skills Instruction

Orion Series Volumes	5 Themes	5 Literary Response Skills	5 Comprehension Skills
Under Attack	Perseverance	Analyze Character	Determining Importance
First Encounter	Courage	Analyze Plot	Comparing and Contrasting
Betrayed	Respect	Analyze Setting	Finding Cause and Effect
Deception	Integrity	Analyze Irony	Making Inferences
Countdown	Responsibility	Flashback	Identifying Theme

Connection to Grade-Level Literature Through Literary Themes

The five universal themes in each *Impact Graphic Novels* series connect to more complex literature. The teacher's guides offer suggested titles from core reading curriculum and examples of how to make the thematic connection.

Perseverance
- *The Two Towers*, J. R. R. Tolkien
- *How I Found the Strong*, Margaret McMullen

Courage
- *The Iliad*, Homer
- *Soldier's Heart*, Gary Paulsen

Respect
- *The Merchant of Venice*, William Shakespeare
- *The Light in the Forest*, Conrad Richter

Integrity
- *Death of a Salesman*, Arthur Miller
- *Lily's Crossing*, Patricia Reilly Giff

Responsibility
- *Les Miserables*, Victor Hugo
- *Number the Stars*, Lois Lowry

These Stories Make a Positive Impact!

Your students will be motivated and inspired by what the *Impact* characters go through, the challenges they overcome, and the lessons they learn.

Clear Instruction With Meaningful Independent Work

Simple, easy-to-follow instruction and independent study opportunities make this reading series ideal for teachers, paraprofessionals, or volunteers.

Each series includes:
- 5 student volumes
- 1 teacher's guide

Instructional Path

Set the Scene

Focus on Literary Response

Students learn and practice one key literary response skill.

Each section has the same structure:

Teach Direct instruction and modeling of skills provides the foundation for learning.

Read Paired, silent reading time provides support for a variety of reading levels.

Discuss Student-focused, rich discussion motivates struggling readers to talk about the books.

Write Self-managed blackline masters connect independent work to each day's instruction.

Focus on Comprehension

Students learn and practice one key comprehension skill.

Review and Extend

Students review and practice both literary response and comprehension skills.

Wrap-Up

Impact Teacher's Guides

Students learn literary response skills as they talk about the story.

Students connect personally to the theme, characters, and plot. Students also share what they know and like about graphic novels.

Each lesson provides an example of how to accommodate the teaching process for your English language learners.

Lesson 1

Orion *Volume 1*
Under Attack

Summary: Tornadoes destroy skyscrapers and gigantic glaciers begin to melt! Something—or someone—is causing chaos on Earth. A handful of unique teenagers have been called upon to save the planet. Can they handle the enormous challenge?

Lesson Overview

Theme: Perseverance
Literary Response Skill: Analyze Character
Comprehension Skill: Determining Importance
Literature Connection: *The Two Towers,* by J. R. R. Tolkien; *How I Found the Strong,* by Margaret McMullan

---

Before Reading

Set the Scene

Connect to Personal Experience
- Ask students to describe a time when they became frustrated while trying to achieve a goal. How did it end up? What were the obstacles they had to overcome?
- Have students give examples of athletes, musicians, and people they know who *persevered,* or kept working hard at something to reach a goal.

Get Motivated
- Tell students they will be reading about a group of teenagers who strive to overcome obstacles and achieve goals as a group. Display a copy of *Under Attack* and ask students what they think the book will be about, based on the cover illustration.
- Distribute copies of *Under Attack.* Turn to the inside front cover and explain the instructions for reading graphic novels. Have students look at the cover, skim the pages, and share their thoughts. Ask: *Have you ever read a graphic novel? Does it remind you of anything else you've read? What do you like about this book? Do you think it will be different from other books you've read in this class?*

About the Characters
- Have students turn to pp. 2–3. Ask a volunteer to read the summary (p. 3). Ask: *What can we tell about these characters? What might their challenges be? Have you experienced any of these challenges?*

During Reading

Focus on Literary Response: Analyze Character

Teach
- Explain that we *analyze characters* in a story through the things the characters say and think, through their actions and appearance, and through the things other characters say or think about them.
- Read aloud Chapter 1, pp. 4–10. Model the following think-aloud: *Ariel snatches the magazine right from under Jon's nose. She also shows off that she's stronger than Jon. I think she's a bully. I wonder if that might cause problems for the others.* Continue the discussion by asking students what they can tell about other characters.

Read
- Pair students of differing abilities to read the rest of Chapter 1. Have partners read four pages silently, signal to the other with a thumbs-up or other silent signal when they're done, and wait quietly for the other to finish. Then each should share a thought or question about a character and discuss it with the partner. Continue in this way until the end of the chapter.

Discuss
- Ask questions to help students analyze the characters from Chapter 1:
  Jon has a lot to live up to with General Davids as a father. Do you think he'll be a good leader?
  What do you think of Leeza's attitude? (p. 23) What does she say that suggests she will help the team overcome hard times?
  What is the Alpha squad's mission? (stop the Sectarians from taking over the planet) How would you feel if you were part of the team?

Write
- Distribute **Skill Master 1: Character Traits** on p. 6. Students should choose a character from Chapter 1 and write the character's name at the top of the page. Have student pairs describe their characters to each other without giving the names. Then students try to guess each other's characters.
- On a separate piece of paper, ask students to write about the character they admire the most. Students should give the reasons why they chose the character, including powers and personality traits.

ELL Support for **English Language Learners**

Point out examples of slang or idiomatic statements from Chapter 1 of *Under Attack:* "mooning over some girl" (p. 7); "knock it off" (p. 10); "cut it out" (p. 13); "dude" (p. 14); "everything's cool now" (p. 14). Ask volunteers to explain the meaning of each.

Skill Master 1

Focus on Comprehension: Determining Importance

Teach
- Explain that in order to understand a story, readers must decide which events and details in the story are important. *Determining importance* helps readers follow the storyline and make predictions about what will happen next.
- Tell students about a recent personal experience, such as attending a concert or spending the afternoon at a mall. Include major, minor, and unrelated details. Have volunteers retell your story, recounting only the important details.

Rich discussions before, during, and after reading drive to a deeper understanding of the storyline and characters.

Students learn comprehension strategies as they talk about the story.

Each lesson provides an example of how to accommodate the teaching process for your students with special needs.

After each teaching moment, students have the opportunity to practice independently using blackline masters.

Skill Master 2

Read
- Have students recall details about the characters and events in Chapter 1.
- Pair students of differing abilities to read Chapter 2. Tell students to concentrate on important events and details. Have partners read four pages silently, signal to the other with a thumbs-up or other silent signal when they're done, and wait quietly for the other to finish. Then each should share a thought or question that comes up while reading. Continue in this way to the end of the chapter.

Discuss
- Ask students questions to help them determine important events and details in Chapter 2:

  How does the team react to Jon being named captain? (p. 25)

  What task does the general give the team? (p. 31) How well does the team do on the task? (pp. 32–36)

  Which team members earn the general's approval? (p. 43) Why? (They work together.)

  What will the team need to do to complete the obstacle course in 30 seconds? (cooperate, work harder, persevere)

Write
- Distribute **Skill Master 2: Determine Importance** on p. 7. Partners may work together to write appropriate information from Chapter 2 under each heading for each set of pages shown.
- On a separate piece of paper, ask students to briefly describe key events in a book, story, television program, or movie in which a character shows perseverance. Remind students to include only important events and significant details that show the character's perseverance.

Review and Extend

Teach
- **Analyze Character** Remind students that writers reveal details about a character through the character's actions, words, and thoughts, as well as through the words and thoughts of other characters in the story. Prompt students to recall and think about specific characters and their traits: *What do we know about each character's personality? What are each character's strengths? What are their weaknesses?*
- **Determining Importance** Remind students that determining important events and details in a story helps one understand what the story is about. Knowing the order in which important events happen can give clues about what will come next. Ask a volunteer to describe important events from Chapter 2. Have other students recall the order in which the events take place.

Read
- Pair students of differing abilities to read Chapter 3. Before they begin, ask students to pay attention to character traits and key events and details. Have partners read four pages silently, signal to the other with a thumbs-up or other silent signal when they're done, and wait quietly for the other to finish. Then each should share a thought or question regarding characters or important events. Students continue in this way to the end of the chapter.

Discuss
- Lead the class in a discussion about the characters and the important events and details in Chapter 3.

  Think about Leeza's personality and actions in Chapter 3. What important events does she have a part in? (encourages the team to listen to Jon; is the object of a joke on Jon)

  Think about Luis's experiences in this chapter. Can you predict an important event later in the team's mission involving Luis? (His visions may identify the traitor and help the team.)

  How does Jon's perseverance throughout the story affect the group's results on the obstacle course? (p. 58–62)

Write
- Distribute copies of the **Writing Master** on p. 32. Ask students to choose one character that really has to persevere in the story and describe the key events that show the character's perseverance. Have students explain how the character's traits help or hinder the character in reaching his or her goals.

Writing Master

After Reading

Wrap-Up

Discuss
- Allow students to reflect on what they have read.

  Do you know anybody like Jon, Ariel, Leeza, or Kathy? Explain.

  Which character would you most like as a friend? Why?

  Does any character remind you of yourself? Explain.

  Have you ever been on a team or part of a group? Did you work together? Did you reach your team goals?

📖 Connect to Literature

Connect the theme of perseverance to other classroom literature, such as Tolkien's *The Two Towers* or McMullan's *How I Found the Strong*. For example:

- *In The Two Towers, Frodo and Sam make a dangerous journey, helping each other along the way. They risk their lives to take the ring to Mordor so that it doesn't fall into evil hands. Frodo and Sam show perseverance. Which characters in Under Attack persevere? How are their situations similar to Frodo and Sam's? How are they different?*

- *In How I Found the Strong, Frank "Shanks" Russell resents having to stay home while his father and brother fight in the Civil War. Then he realizes that feeling sorry for himself doesn't make things better. He perseveres by working with Buck, a slave, to provide for the family during the war. This attitude helps him through a dangerous mission to win Buck's freedom. How is Jon's situation in Under Attack similar to Frank's? How is it different?*

Relates the literary response skill to the comprehension skill, using the lesson theme.

Discussions are framed around students' personal response to the characters. This springboards into discussion about a similar theme in a **grade-level literary selection**.

Orion *Volume 1*
Under Attack

Summary: Tornadoes destroy skyscrapers and gigantic glaciers begin to melt! Something—or someone—is causing chaos on Earth. A handful of unique teenagers have been called upon to save the planet. Can they handle the enormous challenge?

Lesson Overview

Theme: Perseverance

Literary Response Skill: Analyze Character

Comprehension Skill: Determining Importance

Literature Connection: *The Two Towers,* by J. R. R. Tolkien; *How I Found the Strong,* by Margaret McMullan

Before Reading

Set the Scene

Connect to Personal Experience

- Ask students to describe a time when they became frustrated while trying to achieve a goal. How did it end up? What were the obstacles they had to overcome?

- Have students give examples of athletes, musicians, and people they know who *persevered,* or kept working hard at something to reach a goal.

Get Motivated

- Tell students they will be reading about a group of teenagers who strive to overcome obstacles and achieve goals as a group. Display a copy of *Under Attack* and ask students what they think the book will be about, based on the cover illustration.

- Distribute copies of *Under Attack.* Turn to the inside front cover and explain the instructions for reading graphic novels. Have students look at the cover, skim the pages, and share their thoughts. Ask: *Have you ever read a graphic novel? Does it remind you of anything else you've read? What do you like about this book? Do you think it will be different from other books you've read in this class?*

About the Characters

- Have students turn to pp. 2–3. Ask a volunteer to read the summary (p. 3). Ask: *What can we tell about these characters? What might their challenges be? Have you experienced any of these challenges?*

Focus on Literary Response: Analyze Character

Teach

- Explain that we *analyze characters* in a story through the things the characters say and think, through their actions and appearance, and through the things other characters say or think about them.

- Read aloud Chapter 1, pp. 4–10. Model the following think-aloud: *Ariel snatches the magazine right from under Jon's nose. She also shows off that she's stronger than Jon. I think she's a bully. I wonder if that might cause problems for the others.* Continue the discussion by asking students what they can tell about other characters.

Read

- Pair students of differing abilities to read the rest of Chapter 1. Have partners read four pages silently, signal to the other with a thumbs-up or other silent signal when they're done, and wait quietly for the other to finish. Then each should share a thought or question about a character and discuss it with the partner. Continue in this way until the end of the chapter.

Discuss

- Ask questions to help students analyze the characters from Chapter 1:

  Jon has a lot to live up to with General Davids as a father. Do you think he'll be a good leader?

  What do you think of Leeza's attitude? (p. 23) What does she say that suggests she will help the team overcome hard times?

  What is the Alpha squad's mission? (stop the Sectaurians from taking over the planet) How would you feel if you were part of the team?

Write

- Distribute **Skill Master 1: Character Traits** on p. 6. Students should choose a character from Chapter 1 and write the character's name at the top of the page. Have student pairs describe their characters to each other without giving the names. Then students try to guess each other's characters.

- On a separate piece of paper, ask students to write about the character they admire the most. Students should give the reasons why they chose the character, including powers and personality traits.

Skill Master 1

....

Focus on Comprehension: Determining Importance

Teach

- Explain that in order to understand a story, readers must decide which events and details in the story are important. *Determining importance* helps readers follow the storyline and make predictions about what will happen next.

- Tell students about a recent personal experience, such as attending a concert or spending the afternoon at a mall. Include major, minor, and unrelated details. Have volunteers retell your story, recounting only the important details.

Read

- Have students recall details about the characters and events in Chapter 1.

- Pair students of differing abilities to read Chapter 2. Tell students to concentrate on important events and details. Have partners read four pages silently, signal to the other with a thumbs-up or other silent signal when they're done, and wait quietly for the other to finish. Then each should share a thought or question that comes up while reading. Continue in this way to the end of the chapter.

Discuss

- Ask students questions to help them determine important events and details in Chapter 2:

    How does the team react to Jon being named captain? (p. 25)

    What task does the general give the team? (p. 31) How well does the team do on the task? (pp. 32–36)

    Which team members earn the general's approval? (p. 43) Why? (They work together.)

    What will the team need to do to complete the obstacle course in 30 seconds? (cooperate, work harder, persevere)

Write

- Distribute **Skill Master 2: Determine Importance** on p. 7. Partners may work together to write appropriate information from Chapter 2 under each heading for each set of pages shown.

- On a separate piece of paper, ask students to briefly describe key events in a book, story, television program, or movie in which a character shows perseverance. Remind students to include only important events and significant details that show the character's perseverance.

Support for Students with Special Needs

Allow students more time to discuss and expand on the discussion questions. Ask: *How do Thom, Ariel, Luis, Kathy, and Naveen try to complete the obstacle course? (pp. 32–37) How do their attempts compare with Jon and Leeza's? (pp. 38–41)*

Skill Master 2

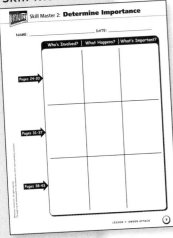

Review and Extend

Teach

- **Analyze Character** Remind students that writers reveal details about a character through the character's actions, words, and thoughts, as well as through the words and thoughts of other characters in the story. Prompt students to recall and think about specific characters and their traits: *What do we know about each character's personality? What are each character's strengths? What are their weaknesses?*

- **Determining Importance** Remind students that determining important events and details in a story helps one understand what the story is about. Knowing the order in which important events happen can give clues about what will come next. Ask a volunteer to describe important events from Chapter 2. Have other students recall the order in which the events take place.

Read

- Pair students of differing abilities to read Chapter 3. Before they begin, ask students to pay attention to character traits and key events and details. Have partners read four pages silently, signal to the other with a thumbs-up or other silent signal when they're done, and wait quietly for the other to finish. Then each should share a thought or question regarding characters or important events. Students continue in this way to the end of the chapter.

Discuss

- Lead the class in a discussion about the characters and the important events and details in Chapter 3.

  Think about Leeza's personality and actions in Chapter 3. What important events does she have a part in? (encourages the team to listen to Jon; is the object of a joke on Jon)

  Think about Luis's experiences in this chapter. Can you predict an important event later in the team's mission involving Luis? (His visions may identify the traitor and help the team.)

  How does Jon's perseverance throughout the story affect the group's results on the obstacle course? (p. 58–62)

Write

- Distribute copies of the **Writing Master** on p. 32. Ask students to choose one character that really has to persevere in the story and describe the key events that show the character's perseverance. Have students explain how the character's traits help or hinder the character in reaching his or her goals.

Writing Master

After Reading

Wrap-Up

Discuss

- Allow students to reflect on what they have read.

  Do you know anybody like Jon, Ariel, Leeza, or Kathy? Explain.

  Which character would you most like as a friend? Why?

  Does any character remind you of yourself? Explain.

  Have you ever been on a team or part of a group? Did you work together? Did you reach your team goals?

Connect to Literature

Connect the theme of perseverance to other classroom literature, such as Tolkien's *The Two Towers* or McMullan's *How I Found the Strong*. For example:

- *Frodo and Sam in* The Two Towers *make a dangerous journey, helping each other along the way. They risk their lives to take the ring to Mordor so that it doesn't fall into evil hands. Frodo and Sam show perseverance. Which characters in* Under Attack *persevere? How are their situations similar to Frodo and Sam's? How are they different?*

- *In* How I Found the Strong, *Frank "Shanks" Russell resents having to stay home while his father and brother fight in the Civil War. Then he realizes that feeling sorry for himself doesn't make things better. He perseveres by working with Buck, a slave, to provide for the family during the war. This attitude helps him through a dangerous mission to win Buck's freedom. How is Jon's situation in* Under Attack *similar to Frank's? How is it different?*

STECK-VAUGHN
IMPACT
GRAPHIC NOVELS

NAME: _____ DATE: _____

Character's Name

How does this character act?

What do the other characters say or think about this character?

How does this character get along with other characters?

Would you want this character on your team? Why or why not?

NAME: _____ DATE: _____

Who's Involved?	What Happens?	What's Important?
Pages 24–30		
Pages 31–37		
Pages 38–43		

Orion *Volume 2*
First Encounter

Summary: Team Alpha blasts off on a mission to protect Earth from a second wave of alien attacks. It's a dangerous mission to destroy the aliens' satellites. Along the way, the team's ship is damaged, the other Orion ships lose power, and a Sectaurian gets aboard the Alpha ship!

Lesson Overview

Theme: Courage

Literary Response Skill: Analyze Plot

Comprehension Skill: Comparing and Contrasting

Literature Connection: *The Iliad,* by Homer; *Soldier's Heart,* by Gary Paulsen

Before Reading ....

Set the Scene

Connect to Personal Experience

• Ask students to talk about a time when they had to be *courageous*—brave or emotionally strong—in the face of a problem.

• Have students give examples of famous people who faced a dangerous or difficult challenge and came out on top.

Get Motivated

• Tell students that in this book, the members of Team Alpha must battle alien forces to disable the equipment that is destroying the earth. Hold up a copy of *First Encounter* and ask what they think the book will be about.

• Distribute copies of *First Encounter.* Have students look at the cover, skim the pages, and share what they think is going to happen.

About the Characters

• Turn to pp. 2–3. Have a volunteer read the summary (p. 3). *What do the character summaries and story summary tell us about the characters? How will the characters react in the face of danger?*

Focus on Literary Response: Analyze Plot

Teach

- *Plot* is the series of related events that make up a story. Plot answers the question *What happens?* It usually starts with a conflict, or problem. It also includes a climax, the most exciting part of the story as characters try to solve the conflict. The resolution is when the problem is solved and the story ends.

- Read aloud Chapter 1, pp. 4–6. Model a think-aloud: *Jon's dad says, "The future of the human race depends on your ability to lead the team on this mission." That's a lot of pressure! Jon looks confident, but he must be scared, too. I wonder how Jon's going to deal with it.*

Read

- Pair students of differing abilities to read the rest of Chapter 1. Have partners read four pages silently, signal to the other with a thumbs-up or other silent signal when they're done, and wait quietly for the other to finish. Then each partner shares a thought about the most important events in the story so far. Continue in this way to the end of the chapter.

Discuss

- Ask questions to help students gain an understanding of the plot:

  What is the main, earth-shattering conflict of the plot that requires the team to show great courage? (pp. 4–5)

  On pages 6–9, Team Alpha discusses the dangerous mission to disable the aliens' satellites. What are some of their challenges? (They could set off the satellites, Jon doubts his leadership abilities, and some team members don't get along.)

Write

- Distribute **Skill Master 3: Story Sequence Chart** on p. 12. Have partners complete parts of the chart with information from Chapter 1. They can add to the story chart as they read Chapters 2 and 3. Some elements, such as the resolution, cannot be completed until later.

- On a separate sheet of paper, have students write a brief prediction of what will happen in the rest of *First Encounter*. Remind them to include complications, a climax, and a resolution. Students may use their Story Sequence Chart as a reference.

Skill Master 3

Skill Master 3: **Story Sequence Chart**

Focus on Comprehension: Comparing and Contrasting

Teach

- Explain that when we *compare* two or more things, such as characters or events, we look at how they are similar. When we *contrast* two or more elements in a story, we look at how they are different.

- Compare and contrast two well-known actors, athletes, or singers. Draw a Venn diagram on the board and label each circle with a celebrity's name. Ask students to think of characteristics of each celebrity and have a volunteer record these in the circles. Any shared characteristics should be listed in the overlapping section.

Skill Master 4

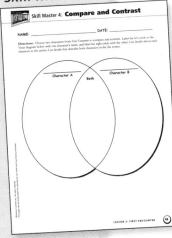

Read

- Ask a volunteer to recall what happened in Chapter 1.

- Pair students of differing abilities to read Chapter 2. Ask them to focus on two characters' strengths and weaknesses. Have partners read four pages silently, signal to the other with a thumbs-up or other silent signal when they're done, and wait quietly for the other to finish. Then each partner shares a thought about the two characters they chose—how they are alike and different. Continue in this way to the end of the chapter.

Discuss

- Ask questions to help students compare and contrast characters:

  How does Kathy's conversation with her parents compare to Ariel's? How does Ariel's conversation compare with Jon's? How do the attitudes of the parents contrast? (pp. 33–35)

  What comparison does Jon make about his parents? (p. 37) What do you think his mother would have said to encourage him if she were alive? What would his father most likely say?

Write

- Distribute **Skill Master 4: Compare and Contrast** on p. 13. Have partners fill in each field of the Venn diagram with details from Chapter 2 to complete the activity. Ask volunteers to share elements of their completed diagrams.

- On a separate sheet of paper, have students write two brief paragraphs comparing and contrasting two people they know. Encourage them to use a Venn diagram to organize their ideas before writing.

Review and Extend

Teach

- **Analyze Plot** Remind students that the events in a story make up the plot. All plots have a conflict that is resolved by the end of the story. Help students remember the important events that make up the plot so far: *What are some of the problems in Chapters 1 and 2?*

- **Comparing and Contrasting** Remind students that when we compare and contrast we look at similarities and differences. Name a character from a well-known movie or book. Ask students to choose someone from *First Encounter* who is most like that character and explain why. How are they different?

Read

- Pair students of differing abilities to read Chapter 3. Remind students to pay attention to how the conflict of the story is resolved. Have partners read four pages silently, signal to the other with a thumbs-up or other silent signal when they're done, and wait quietly for the other to finish. Then each partner shares a clue about how they think the conflict will be resolved. Continue in this way to the end of the chapter.

Discuss

- Ask questions to help students undertand elements of the story:

    What event would you say is the climax of the story? (destroying the satellite and escaping with mere seconds to spare)

    How does the real ending of the story compare to how you thought it was going to end?

    How does Jon's courage help pull the team together? (pp. 47–48)

Write

- Distribute copies of the **Writing Master** on p. 32. Ask students to choose one character from *First Encounter* who exhibits courage and describe key events that show that character's courage. Have students tell how the character's traits help or hinder the character in reaching his or her goals.

Writing Master

After Reading ⋯⋯⋯⋯⋯⋯⋯⋯⋯⋯⋯⋯⋯⋯⋯⋯⋯⋯⋯

Wrap-Up

Discuss

- Allow students to reflect on what they have read.

    What do you think of Ariel's behavior and attitude throughout the story?

    Which characters show the most courage in the face of danger? How do you think you would react in a similar situation?

    Do you know anyone like Naveen, who jokes about everything?

    Which of the characters is most like you?

Connect to Literature

Connect the theme of courage to other classroom literature, such as Homer's *The Iliad* or Paulsen's *Soldier's Heart.* For example:

- *In Homer's* The Iliad, *Greek soldiers attack the city of Troy. In* First Encounter, *aliens attack Earth. Important figures from both stories are called upon to defend their people and homes. In what ways do the heroes of both stories, Achilles in* The Iliad *and Jon in* First Encounter, *show great courage in the face of danger?*

- *In Paulsen's* Soldier's Heart, *Charley Goddard, a 15-year-old, leaves his farm to fight in the Civil War. Even though he is young, he is courageous and enthusiastic. However, he learns that war is difficult and horrifying. He returns home much older and wiser. Which character in* First Encounter *does Charley Goddard remind you of? What does the character from* First Encounter *learn?*

NAME: _____ DATE: _____

Directions: Write the names of the main characters. For setting, write down where the story happens. Don't forget where the characters all met! Then fill in the rest of the story's plot.

Characters (who):   Setting (where):

Major Conflict (problem):

Event (detail):

Event (detail):

Climax (characters try to solve the problem):

Resolution (after they solve the problem):

Skill Master 4: **Compare and Contrast**

NAME: _____ DATE: _____

Directions: Choose two characters from *First Encounter* to compare and contrast. Label the left circle in the Venn diagram below with one character's name, and label the right circle with the other. List details about each character in the circles. List details that describe both characters in the the center.

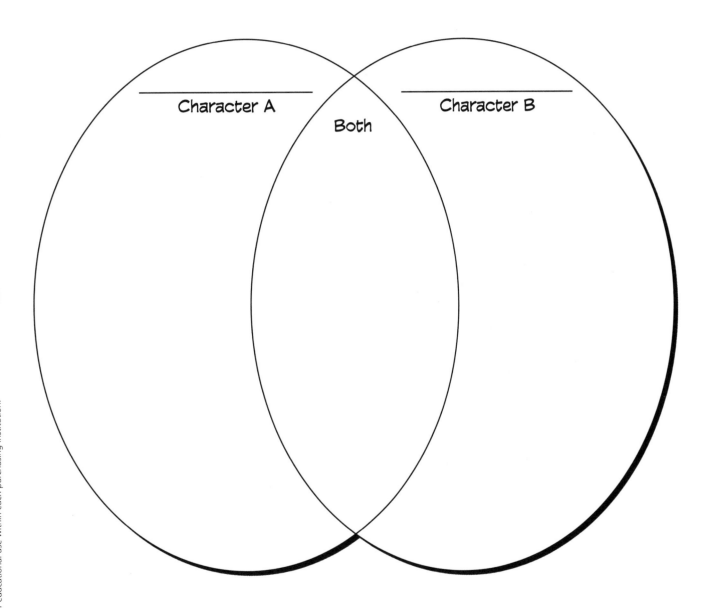

Character A   Both   Character B

Orion *Volume 3*
Betrayed

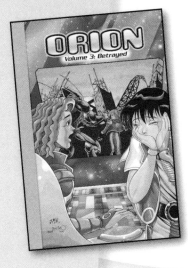

Summary: One alien satellite has been destroyed, but others remain. In order to dismantle the satellites in time, the members of Team Alpha must combine their powers using the Novashield. But Ariel's angry outburts ruin their attempts. Will Luis's disturbing visions about Ariel become reality?

Lesson Overview

Theme: Respect

Literary Response Skill: Analyze Setting

Comprehension Skill: Finding Cause and Effect

Literature Connection: *The Merchant of Venice,* by William Shakespeare; *The Light in the Forest,* by Conrad Richter

Before Reading

Set the Scene

Connect to Personal Experience

- Ask students about a time when they had to work hard to prove themselves to someone. What sorts of things did they have to do? How did they feel about themselves afterward?

- Have students give examples of the types of people they *respect,* or admire and think highly of, and some they don't. Focus the discussion on the personality traits they respect in others and those traits they do not respect.

Get Motivated

- Tell students that in *Betrayed,* Ariel's lack of respect for the others appears to be getting out of control.

- Distribute copies of *Betrayed.* Have students look at the cover, skim the pages, and share their thoughts and predictions about the novel.

About the Characters

- Turn to pp. 2–3. Have a volunteer read the summary (p. 3). Ask: *What do you think Ariel might do to put the team in danger?*

Focus on Literary Response: Analyze Setting

Teach

• Explain that the *setting* of a story is the time and place in which the story happens. The setting creates the mood of the story. In graphic novels, the setting is described in pictures and words.

• Read aloud Chapter 1, pp. 4–12. Model the following think-aloud: *This story takes place on a spaceship in outer space. There isn't really anywhere for the characters to be alone and think about things that are bothering them. I wonder how much the setting has to do with Ariel's bad mood and the lack of respect she shows for the others?*

Read

• Pair students of differing abilities to read the rest of Chapter 1. Have partners read four pages silently, signal to the other with a thumbs-up or other silent signal when they're done, and wait quietly for the other to finish. Then each partner shares a thought about the different settings in Chapter 1. Continue in this way to the end of the chapter.

Discuss

• Ask questions to help students gain an understanding of setting and its effect on the story:

   Do you think the characters act differently in the relaxed setting of the recreation room then in the ship's control room? (pp. 5–6)

   If the team members weren't on a spaceship, how might the mood or atmosphere of the story change?

   Ariel seems to be blowing up often. Do you think she would act differently in a different situation?

Write

• Distribute **Skill Master 5: Setting** on p. 18. Students may work with partners to complete the chart. Have students share elements of their completed charts with the class.

• On a separate sheet of paper, ask students to write a brief summary of Chapter 1, focusing on how the setting affects the events in the story and the characters' actions. Students may use details from their completed charts to help them write their summaries.

Skill Master 5

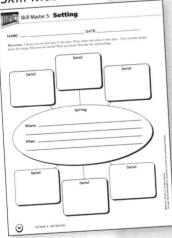

Focus on Comprehension: Finding Cause and Effect

Teach

• When we look for the *effect,* we are looking for "what happens." The *cause* is "why it happens."

• Recount the plot of a recent episode of a popular TV show, or ask a volunteer to do it. Ask students to describe the causes of the things that happened.

Skill Master 6

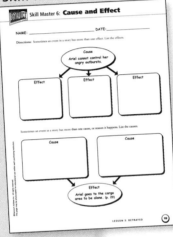

Read

- Have students summarize key events in Chapter 1 of *Betrayed*.

- Pair students of differing abilities to read Chapter 2, urging students to pay attention to causes and effects of things that happen. Have partners read four pages silently, signal to the other with a thumbs-up or other silent signal when they're done, and wait quietly for the other to finish. Then each partner shares a thought about a cause or an effect. Continue in this way to the end of the chapter.

Discuss

- Ask questions to help students find cause-effect relationships in Chapter 2:

  What are the reasons Ariel gives for being so angry all the time? (pp. 24–25) Do you think she's right to disrespect Jon?

  When Ariel first sees the alien on board, why doesn't she call for help? (p. 31)

  What effect does talking with the Sectaurian have on Ariel? (p. 43) What do you think she's going to do? What would you do?

Write

- Distribute **Skill Master 6: Cause and Effect** on p. 19. Students may work with partners to complete the activity. Have volunteers share their completed webs.

- On a separate sheet of paper, ask students to write a brief summary of the causes and effects of the important events in Chapter 2. Students may use their completed webs for reference.

Review and Extend

Teach

- **Analyze Setting** Remind students that setting refers to where and when a story takes place. Help students understand how the setting of the story affects Jon, Thom, and Ariel. Their personalities and powers require lots of open space and time on their own, but they're confined to a spaceship.

- **Finding Cause and Effect** Remind students that *effect* is "what happens" and *cause* is "why it happens." Ask a volunteer to recall key events that happened in Chapter 2 of *Betrayed*. Ask other students why these events happened and/or what happened as a result.

Read

- Pair students of differing abilities to read Chapter 3. Have partners read four pages silently, signal to the other with a thumbs-up or other silent signal when they're done, and wait quietly for the other to finish. Then each partner shares a thought about what they read. Continue in this way to the end of the chapter.

Discuss

- Ask questions to help students understand setting and cause-effect relationships:

  A new setting is introduced in Chapter 3. What is it? (p. 49)

  What do you think might happen in the next volume as a result of Ariel's actions?

  How does Ariel's lack of respect put the team, and the entire Earth, in danger?

Write

- Distribute copies of the **Writing Master** on p. 32. Have students pick one character they respect in *Betrayed* and write about what that character does to earn the respect of the other team members. How does the character show respect for the others? Does the character's behavior help the character reach his or her goals?

Writing Master

After Reading

Wrap-Up

Discuss

- Allow students to reflect on what they have read.

  Do any of the characters remind you of yourself or someone you know?

  What do you like best about Jon as a leader? What do you like least? What could he do better in his role as leader?

  Whose fault do you think it is that the team members in Betrayed *are not getting along? Why are they having a hard time respecting and trusting each other?*

Connect to Literature

Connect the theme of respect to other classroom literature, such as Shakespeare's *The Merchant of Venice* or Richter's *The Light in the Forest*. For example:

- *Shylock, the moneylender in Shakespeare's* The Merchant of Venice, *is an angry, hateful person. He feels disrespected by everyone and vows to have his revenge. The other characters appear to disrespect Shylock in part because of his hatefulness. In what ways does Shylock remind you of Ariel?*

- *True Son, the main character in Richter's* The Light in the Forest, *is a teen without a home who feels caught between two worlds. He is angry and depressed when he is forced to leave the family who raised him and return to his original parents. However, he eventually betrays both families and loses their respect forever. Which character in* Betrayed *reminds you of True Son? How are their stories similar? How are they different?*

Skill Master 5: **Setting**

NAME: _____ DATE:_____

Directions: Choose your favorite part of the story. Write where and when it takes place. Then describe details

Detail

Detail

Detail

Setting

Where: _____

_____

When: _____

_____

Detail

Detail

Detail

NAME: _____ DATE:_____

Directions: Sometimes an event in a story has more than one effect. List the effects.

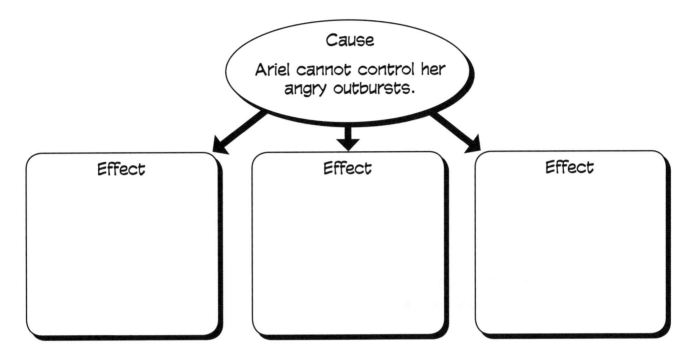

Cause

Ariel cannot control her angry outbursts.

Effect

Effect

Effect

Sometimes an event in a story has more than one cause, or reason it happens. List the causes.

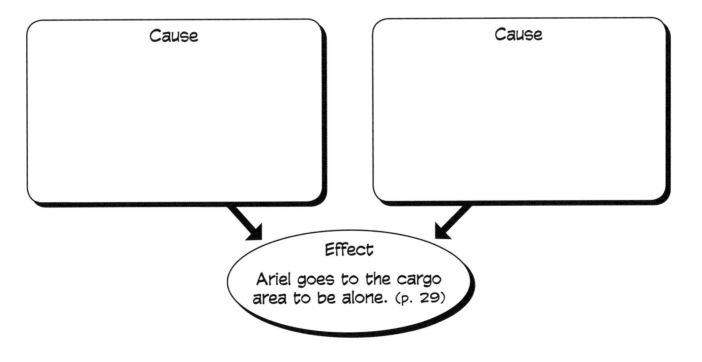

Cause

Cause

Effect

Ariel goes to the cargo area to be alone. (p. 29)

Orion *Volume 4*
Deception

Summary: Team Alpha is shocked that Ariel has joined the evil Sectaurians. When the team enters the Sectaurian city to get Ariel back, Luis's vision comes true, but not like he expected. To save Earth, Team Alpha must first save one of their own!

Lesson Overview

Theme: Integrity

Literary Response Skill: Analyze Irony

Comprehension Skill: Making Inferences

Literature Connection: *Death of a Salesman,* by Arthur Miller; *Lily's Crossing,* by Patricia Reilly Giff

Before Reading

Set the Scene

Connect to Personal Experience

• Ask students to talk about a time when they did the right thing when it wasn't easy to do so.

• Explain that people with *integrity* often choose the difficult path of doing the right thing. Have students give examples of athletes, musicians, or people they know who have integrity.

Get Motivated

• Tell students that in *Deception,* some team members face situations in which their integrity is tested as they battle alien forces.

• Distribute copies of *Deception.* Turn to the inside front cover and go over the instructions for reading graphic novels. Have students look at the cover, skim the pages, and share their thoughts and predictions about what will happen in this volume.

About the Characters

• Have students turn to pp. 2–3. Ask a volunteer to read the summary (p. 3). *How do you think Team Alpha will handle Ariel's betrayal? What other obstacles will Team Alpha have to overcome to save Earth?*

Focus on Literary Response: Analyze Irony

Teach

- Explain that *irony* is the difference between what is expected and what really happens. Offer examples of irony in everyday life to help students understand the concept: *Today's technology—such as computers—is meant to simplify our lives. Just when I think I've mastered a software program, however, a new program is released that makes the old one obsolete. I didn't expect the computer to be so complicated, especially when it's supposed to simplify everything.*

- Read aloud Chapter 1, pp. 4–9. Model the following think-aloud: *Naveen jokes about Ariel's betrayal. I think he's using humor to hide his feelings. Do you think Naveen feels betrayed by Ariel?* Continue the discussion by asking what the other characters think of Ariel's betrayal.

Read

- Pair students of differing abilities to read the rest of Chapter 1. Have partners read four pages silently, signal to the other with a thumbs-up or other silent signal when they're done, and wait quietly for the other to finish. Then each partner shares a thought about any unexpected or ironic situations they notice while reading. Continue in this way to the end of the chapter.

Discuss

- Ask questions to help students gain an understanding of irony:

  On page 6, does it seem like Leeza knows more than she's saying about Ariel? Should she tell what she knows? Why or why not?

  Luis's vision of Ariel shows her lashing out at someone. Do you think his visions are reliable? (p. 14)

  After Jon asks for Luis's help, what does Luis say? (p. 23) Is this what you'd expect?

Write

- Distribute **Skill Master 7: Analyzing Irony** on p. 24. Partners should use details from the story to complete the chart. Ask students to share their responses.

- On a separate sheet of paper, ask students to write down ironic situations from books, movies, or television shows in which they thought one thing was going to happen but another actually did.

> **ELL** Support for **English Language Learners**
>
> Allow students more time to understand the concept of irony. On page 7, when Naveen says Ariel left because "the food on the ship is awful," he doesn't actually expect anyone to believe that. Have volunteers explain why it is ironic that Naveen is joking around at that moment.

Skill Master 7

Skill Master 7: **Analyzing Irony**

NAME: _____ DATE: _____

Directions: Read each sentence. Explain how the sentences describe ironic situations or events.

Example: Kathy says, "I'm sure I . . . err . . . we can still activate the force field."
Irony: *Kathy says "we," but she really thinks she can work the Novashield herself.*

1. Right after the team fails to make the Novashield work, Naveen steals Thom's helmet and makes everyone laugh. (p. 15)
Irony: _____

2. On the spaceship, Thom says that he needs to get some air and then goes for a run around the spaceship. (p. 18)
Irony: _____

3. Jon thinks, "The harder I try to keep control, the worse things get. I can't win!" (p. 22)
Irony: _____

LESSON 4: DECEPTION

Focus on Comprehension: Making Inferences

Teach

- Explain that *inferences* are guesses one makes based on partial information. When an author doesn't say how someone feels, the reader can usually use clues—the tone of a character's voice, a narrowing of the eyes, whether she shouted, thought, or whispered something—to get a better idea of what's really happening.

Skill Master 8

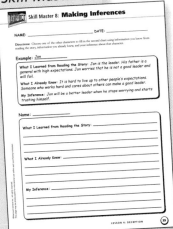

• Describe someone playing a sport without telling the name of the sport. Ask a volunteer to make inferences to decide which sport the person is playing. Then have a volunteer describe a different sport or activity without naming it. Let students guess the sport or activity.

Read

• Have volunteers summarize what happens in Chapter 1.

• Pair students of differing abilities to read Chapter 2. Have partners read four pages silently, signal to the other with a thumbs-up or other silent signal when they're done, and wait quietly for the other to finish. Then each partner shares an inference they made while reading. Continue in this way to the end of Chapter 2.

Discuss

• Ask students questions to help them make inferences about characters and events:

> *After Antilion shows Ariel what he plans for Earth, what can you tell about his concern for humans? (p. 32)*

> *Leeza tells Team Alpha, "It's time you all learn the truth . . . about Ariel."* (p. 38) *What do you assume Leeza knows?* (the reason why Ariel betrayed her team)

Write

• Distribute **Skill Master 8: Making Inferences** on p. 25. Have student partners complete the activity. Ask volunteers to share their inferences.

• On a separate sheet of paper, ask students to describe a key scene in a well-known movie, book, or television program without naming the scene or the work. Let other students guess what the scene is and where it came from.

Review and Extend

Teach

• **Analyze Irony** Remind students that irony is the difference between what is expected and what actually happens. Ask students to share ironic situations from *Deception* or from their own lives.

• **Making Inferences** Remind students that making inferences is using clues in a story to make educated guesses about characters or events. Ask a volunteer to tell what he or she thinks will happen with the Novashield. Have the student state clues or hints from the text that support this prediction.

Read

• Pair students of differing abilities to read Chapter 3. Have partners read four pages silently, signal to the other with a thumbs-up or other silent signal when they're done, and wait quietly for the other to finish. Then each partner shares a thought or question they had while reading. Continue in this way to the end of Chapter 3.

Discuss

- Ask questions to help students gain an understanding of irony and making inferences:

   Ariel never responds well to authority. When Commander Antilion tells her to go to her room, what would you expect her to do? (p. 54)

   What clues tell you that Ariel's betrayal isn't what it seems? (p. 57)

   In this chapter, we find out that Ariel didn't betray her team or her planet. What do you think about her integrity now?

Write

- Distribute copies of the **Writing Master** on p. 32. Ask students to choose one character who shows integrity in the story. Have the students describe key events that show the character's honesty and reliability. Ask students to tell how integrity helps or hinders the character in reaching his or her goals.

After Reading

Wrap-Up

Discuss

- Allow students to reflect on what they have read.

   Would you like to have Ariel as a friend? Why or why not?

   Is Ariel wrong in not telling Team Alpha her plans?

   Do you think Antilion does the right thing for his fellow aliens by planning to take over and destroy Earth? Why or why not?

   Why do you think General Waterman lets the team argue all the time?

   Have you ever been betrayed by a friend? Is that person still your friend?

Connect to Literature

Connect the theme of integrity to other classroom literature, such as Miller's *Death of a Salesman* or Giff's *Lily's Crossing.* For example:

- *Instead of teaching his sons the value of hard work and honesty, Willy, in* Death of a Salesman, *encourages them to be well-liked, to disregard authority, and to steal. Willy obviously doesn't value integrity. Biff realizes that his father's values are wrong. Which characters in* Deception *remind you of Willy and Biff?*

- *In* Lily's Crossing, *Lily and Albert form a close friendship, but they keep many secrets from each other. Which characters in* Deception *are keeping secrets? Does this show integrity or a lack of integrity? How are the characters in* Deception *different from Lily?*

NAME: _____ DATE: _____

Directions: Read each sentence. Explain how the sentences describe ironic situations or events.

Example: Kathy says, "I'm sure I . . . err . . . we can still activate the force field."

Irony: *Kathy says "we," but she really thinks she can work the Novashield herself.*

1. Right after the team fails to make the Novashield work, Naveen tells a joke and makes everyone laugh. (p. 15)

   Irony: _____

   _____

   _____

2. On the spaceship, Thom says that he needs to get some air and then goes for a run around the spaceship. (p. 18)

   Irony: _____

   _____

   _____

3. Jon thinks, "The harder I try to stay in control, the worse things get. I can't win!" (p. 22)

   Irony: _____

   _____

   _____

NAME: _____ DATE: _____

Directions: Choose one of the other characters to fill in the second chart using information you know from reading the story, information you already knew, and your inference about that character.

Example: _Jon_

> What I Learned from Reading the Story: _Jon is the leader. His father is a general with high expectations. Jon worries that he is not a good leader and will fail._
>
> What I Already Knew: _It is hard to live up to other people's expectations. Someone who works hard and cares about others can make a good leader._
>
> My Inference: _Jon will be a better leader when he stops worrying and_

Name: _____

> What I Learned from Reading the Story:
> _____
> _____
> _____
> _____
>
> What I Already Knew: _____
> _____
> _____
> _____
>
> My Inference: _____
> _____
> _____
> _____

Orion *Volume 5*
Countdown

Summary: A Sectaurian ship has rammed the Orion spaceship, injuring General Waterman. The team makes an emergency landing on Earth's moon. The team members get the Novashield working, but they can't prevent the aliens from attacking. Is Earth doomed?

Lesson Overview

Theme: Responsibility

Literary Response Skill: Flashback

Comprehension Skill: Identifying Theme

Literature Connection: *Les Miserables,* by Victor Hugo; *Number the Stars,* by Lois Lowry

Before Reading

Set the Scene

Connect to Personal Experience

- Ask students to talk about a time when they had to show *responsibility,* perhaps by babysitting or helping to stop an argument.

- Have students volunteer examples of people they know who have acted responsibly. Have them also give examples of people who have acted irresponsibly.

Get Motivated

- Hold up a copy of *Countdown* and tell students they will be reading the conclusion of the adventures of Team Alpha.

- Distribute copies of *Countdown.* Have students look at the cover, skim the pages, and share their thoughts and predictions.

About the Characters

- Have students turn to pp. 2–3. Ask a volunteer to read the summary (p. 3). *What will it take for Team Alpha to stop the Sectaurians from destroying Earth?*

Focus on Literary Response: Flashback

Teach

- Explain that a *flashback* is a scene in a story that shows a past event. A flashback can provide background information that gives the reader more insight into the storyline and character motivation.

- Read aloud Chapter 1, pp. 4–9. Model the following think-aloud: *On page 6, Leeza explains to General Waterman why she and Ariel took the risks to trick the Sectaurians. A lot of things could have gone wrong with that plan, but Leeza seems to be taking responsibility for her actions on page 6.*

Read

- Pair students of differing abilities to read the rest of Chapter 1. Have partners read four pages silently, signal to the other with a thumbs-up or other silent signal when they're done, and wait quietly for the other to finish. Then partners share any examples of flashbacks. Students continue in this way to the end of the chapter.

Discuss

- Ask questions to help students gain an understanding of flashback:

    On page 12, Jon thinks back to when his mother was alive. How did Jon's mother die?

    Jon thinks back to the advice his father gave him at the beginning of the mission. (p. 13) General Davids tells Jon to "stay in control." What do we learn about Jon from this flashback? What do we learn about his father, General Davids?

    How does General Davids's advice help Jon in his mission? How does it hurt him?

Write

- Distribute **Skill Master 9: Flashback** on p. 30. Students may work with partners to complete the activity.

- On a separate sheet of paper, ask students to write down examples of flashbacks from their favorite story, movie, or television show. Ask volunteers to read examples.

Skill Master 9

Focus on Comprehension: Identifying Theme

Teach

- Explain that authors frequently suggest an important idea or life lesson in their writing. This is called a *theme*. A theme isn't exactly the same as the moral of a story, but it's similar. A theme usually isn't openly stated. Instead, the reader must think about the elements of the story and make an inference, or educated guess, about the important idea that is being suggested.

- Recount a familiar story and ask volunteers to point out some of the big ideas about life that the author expresses in the story.

Read

- Ask volunteers to recall events and details from Chapter 1.

- Partner students of differing abilities to read Chapter 2. Remind students to look for clues to the story's theme as they read. Have partners read four pages silently, signal to the other with a thumbs-up or other silent signal when they're done, and wait quietly for the other to finish. Then each partner shares an idea about any possible themes they noticed while reading. Continue in this way to the end of Chapter 2.

Discuss

- Ask questions to help students understand the themes revealed in Chapter 2:

  On page 26, Jon rescues Thom. What is the author trying to say about teamwork and leadership by showing Jon taking care of other team members?

  Thom feels a responsibility to help Jon in some way because Jon rescued him. (p. 34) Do you think Jon expects to be repaid for saving Thom?

  What personality trait does General Thorpe show that might contribute to his making bad decisions? (p. 31)

  How do we know that General Davids has emotions after all? (p. 43)

Write

- Distribute **Skill Master 10: What's the Theme?** on p. 31. Have partners complete the activity. Ask volunteers to share some of their responses.

- On a separate sheet of paper, have students write a story based on one of the themes in *Countdown*.

··

Review and Extend

Teach

- **Flashback** Remind students that a flashback is a scene in a story that shows a past event. It usually gives background information so the reader can better understand the storyline or character motivation. Ask: *What do we learn about Jon and his parents from flashbacks?* (Jon often thinks about his father's words, but he respects his mother's advice as well.)

- **Identifying Theme** Remind students that the theme is the important idea suggested in a story. The theme is not usually stated. Instead, readers must make inferences about the important idea the author wants to share. Ask a volunteer to choose a character and recall what happens to this person in Chapter 2. Have other students assist in finding how the character's experiences suggest a theme.

Read

- Pair students of differing abilities to read Chapter 3. Urge students to pay attention to flashbacks and to possible themes. Have partners read four pages silently, signal to the other with a thumbs-up or other silent signal when they're done, and wait quietly for the other to finish. Then each partner shares a thought or a question they had while reading. Continue in this way to the end of Chapter 3.

Skill Master 10

Discuss

- Lead the class in a discussion about flashbacks and themes in Chapter 3:

    On pages 52–53, Team Alpha finally makes the Novashield work. If you could insert a flashback into this scene, what would it be?

    What theme is the author trying to communicate by showing Team Alpha finally getting the Novashield to work? (Some efforts are possible only through teamwork and perseverance.)

Write

- Distribute copies of the **Writing Master** on p. 32. Ask students to choose one character who shows responsibility and describe key events that highlight the character's responsibility. Have students tell how responsibility helps or hinders the character in reaching his or her goals.

Writing Master

After Reading ••

Wrap-Up

Discuss

- Allow students to reflect on what they have read.

    Do you consider Ariel a responsible person early in this series? What do you think of her by the end?

    How does Thom handle stress and fear? Would you handle it the same way?

    Why is teamwork important?

    Which character changes the most?

    Which character acts most responsibly in this book? Would you want him or her as a friend?

Connect to Literature

Connect the theme of responsibility to other classroom literature, such as Hugo's *Les Miserables* or Lowry's *Number the Stars*. For example:

- *In* Les Miserables, *Valjean adopts Cosette, a foster child. By taking on this responsibility, Valjean experiences a dramatic personal change and learns to love and respect others. What characters in* Countdown *experience a similar transformation? How do the characters become more responsible for their actions as the transformation occurs?*

- *In* Number the Stars, *Annemarie Johansen assists her uncle to help people escape from German soldiers during wartime. By safely delivering an important package to her uncle, Annemarie shows that she is very responsible and can be trusted to get a job done. Which characters in* Countdown *can be relied on to get a job done, no matter the risk? How do they show responsibility?*

NAME: _____ DATE: _____

Directions: Choose an example of a flashback from *Countdown* and fill in the boxes with information from the story.

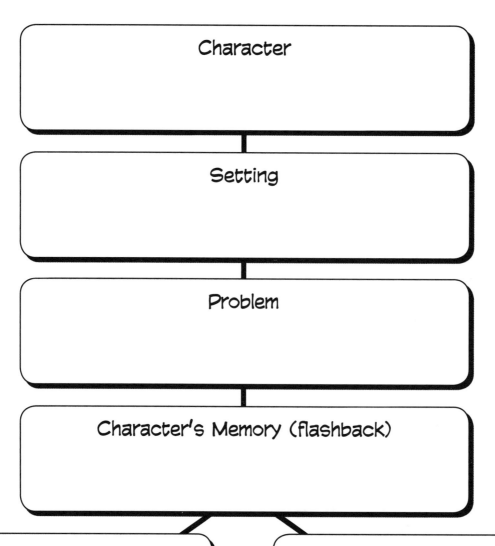

Character

Setting

Problem

Character's Memory (flashback)

What the <u>character</u> learns from the flashback:

What the <u>reader</u> learns from the flashback:

NAME: _____ DATE: _____

Directions: A theme is a story's main idea or message. Pick a character from *Countdown*. Answer the questions below. Then look for the most important word about that character and a possible theme of the story.

What is the character like?

_____

How does he or she change?

_____

What is the character's conflict?

_____

_____

Who is involved in the conflict?

_____

How is the conflict resolved?

_____

_____

What does the character learn from the struggle?

_____

_____

Most important word:

_____

Theme:

_____

_____

Writing Master

NAME: _____ DATE: _____

(character) _____ demonstrates

(lesson theme) _____

when he or she (describe key events) _____

_____

_____

_____

_____

_____

How does (lesson theme) _____ help this

character reach his or her goals? _____

_____

_____

_____

_____

_____

_____

_____

_____

_____

_____

_____

_____